The Story of a Special Day
Volume 61

March 1

60th day of the year
(61st in leap years)
305 days remaining
until the end of the year.

by Michael Dobson

Timespinner Press

Copyright Information

Table of Contents

Cover photograph of Old Faithful by Ansel Adams, for the Event of the Day, Yellowstone National Park Created

March 1 Quotations

"Tomorrow's life is too late. Live today."
— *Martial, born March 1, 40 CE*

"The truth is the light and light is the truth."
— *Ralph Ellison, born March 1, 1913*

"Military cemeteries in every corner of the world are silent testimony to the failure of national leaders to sanctify human life."
— *Yitzhak Rabin, born March 1, 1922*

"Without the hard little bits of marble which are called 'facts' or 'data' one cannot compose a mosaic; what matters, however, are not so much the individual bits, but the successive patterns into which you arrange them, then break them up and rearrange them."
— *Arthur Koestler, died March 1, 1983*

Event of the Day

Yellowstone National Park Created

On March 1, 1872, President Ulysses S. Grant signed the law creating Yellowstone National Park, the first national park in the world.

The Yellowstone region has been inhabited for at least 11,000 years. Clovis Indians mined the large obsidian deposits for arrowheads, and traded them extensively as far away as the Mississippi Valley.

The Lewis and Clark Expedition learned of the Yellowstone region as they passed through Montana in 1805. One of the expedition members, John Colter, left to join a group of fur trappers and passed through the region, encountering at least one geothermal area. He described it as a place of "fire and brimstone," with boiling mud, steaming rivers, and petrified trees, but most listeners considered it a myth.

Some fifty years later, legendary mountain man Jim Bridger visited the region, reporting seeing spouting water and a mountain of glass and yellow rock. Because Bridger was known as a storyteller, his story too was dismissed. It wasn't until 1869 that the region was explored and the stories confirmed.

The amazing Yellowstone ecosystem led to calls to have the region set aside and protected by government. The Hayden Geological Survey prepared a comprehensive report on Yellowstone, complete with photographs and paintings, which helped convince a skeptical Congress that the region was a priceless treasure that should be preserved in its natural state for all time.

There was opposition, of course. Some felt that the regional economy would suffer from federal prohibitions and restrictions, and numerous bills were introduced to allow mining, hunting, and logging. The first park superintendent was given no salary, no funding, and no staff.

The first year, Yellowstone National Park attracted a mere 300 visitors, but in the early 1880s, the railroad came to the area, and tourism began to grow. By 1915, over 1,000 cars per year were entering the park. A constant battle between poachers, tourists, and other usage has been a constant danger to Yellowstone. Earthquakes and fires have also been a source of danger. Today, however, nearly 2 million people visit Yellowstone National Park each year, making it the jewel of the national park system, with such features as Old Faithful Geyser and the Grand Canyon of Yellowstone famous worldwide.

Old Faithful, painted by Albert Bierstadt

March 1 Holidays and Celebrations

Beer Day (Iceland)

Prohibition in Iceland lasted from 1915 to 1935, but "strong beer" (2.25% alcohol or higher) was banned until March 1, 1989. On Beer Day, people take part in a *rúntur* (bar crawl), sometimes lasting until 4:00 am the next day.

Independence Day (Bosnia and Herzegovina)

March 1 is a national public holiday in Bosnia and Herzegovina, celebrating their independence from the Socialist Federal Republic of Yugoslavia in 1992.

Samiljeol (삼일절) (South Korea)

On March 1, 1919, South Koreans made their first public display of resistance to the occupation of the Korean Empire by Japan. While the Samil Movement didn't succeed in overthrowing Japanese rule, it did result in major policy changes, and is celebrated in South Korea each year as a national holiday.

Martenitsa (Bulgaria), Mărţişor (Romania)

Beginning on March 1, Bulgarians exchange and wear white and red tassels or small dolls to welcome the approach of springtime. Each person wears the martenitsa until he or she sees a stork, a swallow, or a blooming tree. In Romania, the tradition is to give a red and white string, worn for twelve days.

Traditional Bulgarian martenitsa

National Pig Day (United States)

The purpose of National Pig Day is "to accord the pig its rightful, though generally

11

unrecognized, place as one of man's most intellectual and domesticated animals." It is celebrated in local areas, primarily in the Midwest.

Roman New Year (Ancient Rome)

In ancient Rome, March 1 marked the beginning of the new year, celebrated with festivals in honor of Mars and Juno and the renewal of the Vestal Fire.

Saint David's Day (Wales)

Welsh tradition claims that Saint David, patron saint of Wales, died March 1, 589, and has been a national day of celebration in Wales since the 18th century.

Welsh Flags, St. David's Day

Festival of Ayyám-i-Há (Bahá'í)

In the Bahá'í calendar, four or five intercalary days synchronize their year to the solar calendar, marked with a festival that lasts from February 26 to March 1. It is sometimes referred to as a Bahá'í Christmas, complete with gift-giving customs.

Christian Feast Days

Saints commemorated on March 1 include Albin, David, Monan, and Suitbert.

What Happened on March 1?

Peter Paul Rubens, *The Rape of the Sabine Women*

752 BCE - Romulus Celebrates the First Roman Triumph

Romulus, legendary first king of Rome, celebrated his victory over the Caeninenses, who had made war against Rome following the Rape of the Sabine Women. From that time, army commanders who achieved notable military success would be granted a triumph by the Roman Senate, consisting of a parade and various religious rites.

1565 CE - Founding of Rio de Janeiro

On March 1, 1565, the Portuguese founded São Sebastião do Rio de Janeiro, in honor of St. Sebastian. It became the capital of Brazil and remained so until the establishment of Brasília in 1960. It is the second largest city in Brazil, and the 26th largest in the world.

Aerial view of Rio de Janeiro

1692 CE - "Salem Witches" Arrested

In the winter of 1692, two young girls, aged 9 and 11, began to exhibit odd behavior. Soon, other young women began to exhibit similar symptoms, but no physical cause was found. Combined with rumors of witchcraft in neighboring villages, this was enough to lead to the arrest, on March 1, 1692, of three women accused of witchcraft: Sara Good, a homeless woman; Sara Osborne, who seldom attended church; and Tituba, a slave. Over 300 people would eventually be implicated as mass hysteria swept the community. Nineteen were hanged and over 150 were imprisoned before the procedures were brought to a halt in May 1693.

"Witchcraft at Salem Village" by William Crafts

1781 CE - Articles of Confederation

On March 1, 1781, the Continental Congress of the United States adopted the Articles of Confederation, the first constitution of the newly independent thirteen colonies. It would be replaced by the U. S. Constitution only eight years later.

1803 CE - Ohio Officially Becomes a State (Retroactively)

In February 1803, President Thomas Jefferson signed an act of Congress approving the boundaries and constitution of the new state of Ohio — but Congress never passed an actual resolution to formally admit Ohio to statehood. In 1953, Congress passed a bill to admit Ohio as a state retroactive to March 1, 1803. The Ohio state legislature approved a new petition for statehood and had it delivered to Washington, DC, by horseback. President Dwight Eisenhower signed the act on August 7, 1953.

1867 CE - Nebraska Becomes a State

On March 1, 1867, the Nebraska Territory was admitted as the 37th state. The state capital was moved from Omaha to Lancaster, renamed

Lincoln in honor of the recently assassinated president.

1868 CE - Pi Kappa Alpha (ΠΚΑ) Founded

The Pi Kappa Alpha fraternity was established on March 1, 1868, at the University of Virginia. Today, the fraternity has over 220 chapters and colonies and over 250,000 initiates in the US and Canada.

1932 CE - Lindbergh Baby Kidnapped

On March 1, 1932, the infant son of Charles and Anne Lindbergh was kidnapped from their New Jersey home, only to be discovered dead a little over two months later. Bruno Richard Hauptmann was found guilty of the kidnapping and was executed by electric chair in 1936.

1954 CE - Hydrogen Bomb Tested

On March 1, 1954, the US detonated the 15 megaton "Castle Bravo" hydrogen bomb at Bikini Atoll in the Pacific. It was the most powerful nuclear device ever tested by the United States. The explosion was nearly three times the expected yield, resulting in the most significant accidental radiological contamination ever caused by the United States.

Castle Bravo thermonuclear explosion

1954 CE - **Capitol Shooting**

On March 1, 1964, four Puerto Rico nationalists shot 30 rounds from automatic pistols in the balcony overlooking the House of Representatives chamber in the United States Capitol, wounding five members of Congress.

1961 CE - Peace Corps Established

On March 1, 1961, President John F. Kennedy issued Executive Order 10924 establishing the Peace Corps. The Peace Corps Act was passed by Congress in September of the same year.

1966 CE - Venera 3 Lands on Venus

On March 1, 1966, the Soviet space probe Venera 3 (Венера-3) crash-landed on the planet Venus, becoming the first spacecraft to land on another planet's surface. Its communication system failed before it could send any information on Venus back to Earth.

1974 CE - "Watergate Seven" Indicted

On March 1, 1974, a grand jury indicted seven men, including several former aides of President Richard Nixon, for conspiracy to hinder the Watergate investigation, and secretly named Nixon as an "unindicted co-conspirator."

Who Was Born on March 1?

The abbreviation "O.S." on some dates refers to the fact that the Russian Empire did not switch from the Julian to the Gregorian calendar at the same time as the rest of Europe, and therefore some figures have two dates for their birth or death.

People whose original names are not in the Western alphabet have their native names in the appropriate script shown in parenthesis.

Art and Literature

William Gaines (March 1, 1922 — June 3, 1992)

William Gaines published EC Comics, initially known for its controversial line of horror and science fiction comics, and subsequently published the highly successful *Mad* Magazine. He was inducted into the Will Eisner Comic

Book Hall of Fame and the Jack Kirby Hall of Fame.

Cover of the first issue of *Mad* Magazine

Robert Lowell (March 1, 1917 — September 12, 1977)

American poet Robert Lowell was the sixth Poet Laureate to the Library of Congress, and won two Pulitzer Prizes, the National Book Award, and the Book Critics Circle Award.

Ralph Ellison (March 1, 1914 — April 16, 1994)

African-American novelist Ralph Ellison is best known for his 1953 novel *Invisible Man,* which won the National Book Award.

William Dean Howells (March 1, 1837 — May 11, 1920)

Author and editor William Dean Howells became known as "the dean of American letters" for his writing and for his tenure as editor of the *Atlantic Monthly.*

Martial (March 1, 40 CE - death uncertain, between 102 and 104 CE)

Latin poet Marcus Valerius Martialis (Martial) is best known for his twelve books of *Epigrams,* short, witty poems that satirize city life in imperial Rome.

Business and Manufacturing

Gil Amelio (March 1, 1943 —)

Technology executive Gil Amelio was CEO of Apple Computers and National Semiconductor.

Movies and Television

Mark-Paul Gosselaar (March 1, 1974 —)

Actor Mark-Paul Gosselaar began as a child star in the television series *Saved by the Bell,* and went on to play in the adult series *NYPD Blue.*

Ron Howard (March 1, 1954 —)

Child star Ron Howard came to fame in the TV sitcoms *The Andy Griffith Show* and *Happy Days,* and subsequently became an acclaimed film director, winning numerous Academy Awards and the 2003 National Medal of Arts.

Ron Howard (right) with Fonzie from *Happy Days*

Catherine Bach (March 1, 1954 —)

Actress Catherine Bach is best known for playing Daisy Duke in the television series *The Dukes of Hazzard*.

Alan Thicke (March 1, 1947 —)

Canadian actor Alan Thicke began as a talk show host and subsequently starred in the TV sitcom *Growing Pains*.

Dirk Benedict (March 1, 1954 —)

Actor Dirk Benedict played "Faceman" in *The A-Team* and Starbuck in the original *Battlestar Galactica*.

Robert Conrad (March 1, 1935 —)

Actor Robert Conrad starred in the television series *The Wild Wild West* and *Baa Baa Black Sheep*.

David Niven (March 1, 1910 — July 29, 1983)

Academy Award winning actor David Niven is perhaps best known for playing Phileas Fogg in *Around the World in Eighty Days* and as the jewel thief in *The Pink Panther*.

Music

Justin Bieber (March 1, 1994 —)

Canadian singer-songwriter Justin Bieber is the first musician to have seven songs from a debut record chart on the Billboard Hot 100. In 2012, *Forbes* magazine named him the third most powerful celebrity in the world. He has sold over 15 million albums to date.

Ke$ha (March 1, 1987 —)

American singer-songwriter and rapper Kesha Rose Sebert has won numerous awards for her electropop sound.

Roger Daltrey (March 1, 1944 —)

Roger Daltrey founded and was the lead singer of the English rock band *The Who*. He appeared in the movie *Tommy* and played Franz Liszt in *Lisztomania*.

Roger Daltrey in performance with The Who

Harry Belafonte (March 1, 1927 —)

Singer Harry Belafonte is known as the "King of Calypso" for his hit "The Banana Boat Song." He is a vocal advocate for civil rights and humanitarian causes.

Glenn Miller (March 1, 1904 — missing in action December 15, 1944)

Big band leader Glenn Miller was known for his many hits including "In the Mood," "Chattanooga Choo Choo," and "A String of Pearls." While traveling to entertain US troops in France during World War II, his plane disappeared in bad weather over the English Channel.

Frédéric Chopin (March 1, 1810(?) — October 17, 1849)

One of the great master of Romantic music, Chopin began composing at the age of seven and performed before the Tsar of Russia at the age of eleven. His many compositions favored the piano as a solo instrument. (He and his family gave his birthdate as March 1, but baptismal records say February 22.)

Politics and Law

Robert Bork (March 1, 1927 —)

Former Solicitor General and appeals court judge Robert Bork was rejected as a nominee for the Supreme Court because of his controversial legal positions. The political term "bork" (to defame someone to prevent appointment to political office) is named for him.

Yitzhak Rabin (יִצְחָק רַבִּין) (March 1, 1922 — November 4, 1995)

Israeli Prime Minister Yitzhak Rabin co-won the 1994 Nobel Peace Prize with Shimon Peres and Yasser Arafat. He was assassinated in 1995.

Yitzhak Rabin, Bill Clinton, and Yasser Arafat

Religion

Cardinal Terence Cooke (March 1, 1921 — October 6, 1983)

Catholic prelate Terence Cooke served as Archbishop of New York from 1968 to his death, and was elevated to Cardinal in 1969. He received the Presidential Medal of Freedom in 1984, and is currently in the canonization process for potential sainthood.

Science and Technology

Deke Slayton (March 1, 1924 — June 13, 1993)

Astronaut Deke Slayton was one of the original Mercury Seven astronauts and served as NASA's director of flight crew operations.

Sports

Ye Shiwen (葉詩文) (March 1, 1996 —)

Chinese swimmer Ye Shiwen won two gold medals in the 2012 Summer Olympics, setting a world record in the 400m event and the Olympic record in the 200m event.

Chris Webber (March 1, 1973 —)

Retired NBA All-Star Chris ("C-Webb") Webber led the University of Michigan Wolverines "Fab Five" to two NCAA Division I basketball championships. He was indicted and stripped of his All-American honors for his involvement in the Ed Martin payoff scandal.

Chris Webber

Elvin Bethea (March 1, 1946 —)

Former Houston Oiler football defensive end Elvin Bethea was elected to the Pro Football Hall of Fame in 2003.

Pete Rozelle (March 1, 1914 — February 18, 1998)

Pete Rozelle was commissioner of the National Football League from 1960 to 1989.

Harry Caray (March 1, 1917 — September 12, 1977)

Sports broadcaster Harry Caray covered Chicago baseball teams the White Sox and the Cubs, becoming well known for leading the fans in singing "Take Me Out to the Ball Game" during the seventh inning stretch and for his trademark exclamation "Holy cow!"

Who Died on March 1?

Actors and Actresses

Joe Besser (August 12, 1907 — March 1, 1988)

Comedian Joe Besser was briefly a member of the Three Stooges. He played Stinky in *The Abbott and Costello Show* and the maintenance man in *The Joey Bishop Show.*

Jackie Coogan (October 26, 1914 — March 1, 1984)

Silent film child star Jackie Coogan played opposite Charlie Chaplin in 1927's *The Kid,* but his exceptional earnings were squandered by his mother and stepfather, leading to the "Coogan Act" to protect child actor income. Later in life, he became known for playing Uncle Fester in TV's *The Addams Family.*

Jackie Coogan (right) with Charlie Chaplin in *The Kid*.

Literature and Words

Arthur Koestler (September 5, 1905 — March 1, 1983)

Hungarian-British author Arthur Koestler wrote the famous anti-totalitarian novel *Darkness at Noon.*

Music

Frank Teschemacher (March 13, 1906 — March 1, 1932)

Jazz clarinet and alto sax player Frank Teschemacher influenced numerous jazz musicians, including Benny Goodman and Pee Wee Russell.

Politics and Espionage

Andrew Breitbart (February 1, 1969 — March 1, 2012)

Conservative activist Andrew Breitbart was an editor for the *Drudge Report* website and played a role in highly edited and controversial political videos involving USDA official Shirley Sherrod and the community group ACORN.

Peter Malkin (צבי מלחין) (May 27, 1927 — March 1, 2005)

Israeli secret agent Peter Malkin was a member of the team that captured Adolf Eichmann in Argentina in 1960 and brought him to trial.

John Haggin (1753 — March 1, 1825)

Famed "Indian fighter" John Haggin was one of the earliest settlers of Kentucky, one of the founders of Lexington, and a leading figure in the movement toward Kentucky statehood.

Record Holders

Pauline Musters (February 26, 1876 — March 1, 1895)

Named by the *Guinness Book of Records* as the shortest woman ever recorded, Pauline Musters measured 23 inches (58 centimeters) tall. Born in the Netherlands, she died in New York City at the age of 19.

Science and Technology

Edwin H. Land (May 7, 1909 — March 1, 1991)

Inventor Edwin H. Land co-founded the Polaroid Corporation and invented the Land Instant Camera. He developed the Retinex theory of color vision and provided assistance to Cold War research in photo intelligence.

Polaroid Land Camera, circa 1969

The month of March, from the illuminated manuscript
Les Très Riches Heures du duc de Berry

March:
The Story of a Month

The Third Month

In ancient Rome, March was the first month of the year. As the first month of spring, in the Mediterranean climate it marked the beginning of the military campaign season. That's why March (Martius) is named in honor of Mars, the Roman god of war.

Although the first month of the year was moved back to January sometime during the transition of Rome from a kingdom to a republic (historians differ), March was the first month of the year in Russia until the end of the 15th Century, and is the first month of the year in many other cultures and religions.

In the northern hemisphere, March 1 marks the beginning of meteorological spring. In the southern hemisphere, March is the equivalent of September, making southern hemisphere March the beginning of autumn.

March is one of the seven months that have 31 days in it. March starts on the same day of the week as November every year, and except for leap years starts on the same day as February. March starts on the same day of the week as the previous June except for leap years, and in leap years starts on the same day as the previous September and December.

March in Other Cultures

In Finland, March is called *maaliskuu* (earthy month). In Ukraine, it's *березень* (birch tree). Other names for March include *Lentmonat* (Saxon), *Hyld-monath* (Angles), and *sušec* (Slovene).

March Symbols

Birthstones

Aquamarine and bloodstone, both representing courage.

Aquamarine

Birth Flowers

Daffodils

Daffodils in
Bagatelle Park,
Paris, France

March Events

Honorary months: Presidents, Congresses, and nations around the world issue proclamations recognizing particular months to honor certain causes. These events generally fall in March. (All US unless otherwise noted.)

- National Nutrition Month

- American Red Cross Month

- Women's History Month (celebrated in Canada during October)

- Irish-American Heritage Month

- Colorectal Cancer Awareness Month

- Fire Prevention Month (The Philippines)

Women's History Month: Suffrage picket line, 1917

"March Madness": (United States) The NCAA Men's Division I Basketball Championship, popularly known as "March Madness" or the "Big Dance," is a single-elimination tournament to establish the champion college basketball team.

Movable events: Some events change dates from year to year.

- **Mardi Gras:** French for "Fat Tuesday," this celebration takes place the day before Ash Wednesday, the beginning of the Lenten season. The New Orleans Mardi Gras celebration is the most famous, but Mardi Gras and the Carnival season (between Ephiphany and Ash Wednesday) are celebrated in many areas with large Catholic populations. Mardi Gras can take place anywhere from February 3 to March 9 in regular years, and from February 4 to March 9 in leap years.

Mardi Gras Night Parade, New Orleans, 2012

- **Casimir Pulaski Day:** (Illinois) The first Monday in March is observed as a holiday in Illinois, in memory of the Revolutionary War cavalry officer born in Poland. Dates range from March 1 to March 7.

March Zodiac Signs

From the perspective of someone on Earth, the Sun appears to move through the sky throughout the year, along a path astronomers call the ecliptic plane. The ecliptic plane is divided into twelve constellations, known as the zodiac, based on traditionally observed patterns of stars. On your birthday, you can't see your constellation, because it's part of the daytime sky.

The zodiac was first developed by Babylonian astronomers about 2,500 years ago. Because they were unaware that the Earth wobbles like a spinning top (a motion known as *precession*), they didn't make allowance for the fact that the Sun's path through the zodiac changes over time.

That means there are now two sets of dates for your birth sign. The *tropical dates* are the original Babylonian dates; the *siderial dates* tell you where the Sun actually appears as it moves along its annual path.

Zodiac signs for March 1 are Aquarius (siderial) and Pisces (tropical).

Aquarius

Tropical January 20 to February 19

Siderial February 12 to March 8 (March 9 in leap years)

Aquarius is one of the oldest recognized constellations, originally representing the Babylonian god Ea. In Latin, Aquarius means "water-carrier," represented in its symbol. In Greek mythology, Aquarius is sometimes associated with Deucalion, who survived a world-cleansing flood. In Chinese astronomy, it is known as the Black Tortoise of the North (北方玄武, Běi Fāng Xuán Wǔ).

In astrology, Aquarius is considered to be masculine and extroverted, and despite the name is an air sign. Aquarians are supposed to be philanthropical, inventive, and individualistic.

Pisces

Tropical February 20 to March 20

Siderial March 15 to April 14

In the Roman legend of Venus and her son Cupid, they escaped the clutches of Typhon, known as the "father of all monsters," by transforming into fish and tying themselves together with rope. That's why the name Pisces is plural for fish. The constellation appears as a somewhat ragged "V" shape, representing the rope, with the "fish" located at the two rope ends.

In astrology, Pisces is a water sign, compatible with the other water signs Cancer and Scorpio, as well as with the earth signs Taurus, Virgo, and Capricorn. Pisceans are supposed to be imaginative, compassionate, unworldly, secretive, and escapist.

What Day of the Week?

On what day of the week does March 1 fall?

Unfortunately, this isn't an easy question. Because the calendar year is 365 days long (366 in leap years), it doesn't divide evenly by the seven days of the week.

Also, the Earth goes around the Sun in about 365-1/4 days, so a calendar tends to drift over time. That's why the same date falls on different weekdays in different years.

This is made even more complicated by a change in calendars that took place in 1582. Our modern calendar has its roots in ancient Rome, in a calendar reform conducted by Julius Caesar. Caesar commissioned mathematicians to attack the problem, and came up with the idea of *leap years*, and thus standardized the calendar for centuries to come. This was called the *Julian calendar.*

Over time, however, the small errors in Caesar's calculation compounded. That's why Pope Gregory XIII commissioned the *Gregorian calendar*, used in most of the world today. Some countries converted in 1582, when the calendar was first developed; some converted later; other still haven't changed.

Gregorian and Julian aren't the only types of calendars. The Hebrew year, the Islamic year, and many other calendars are used in different parts of the world and among different people.

You can convert Gregorian dates to other calendars, including the Hebrew calendar, the Islamic calendar, and even the Mayan calendar by visiting the Fourmilab Calendar Converter at http://www.fourmilab.ch/documents/calendar/.

A 50-year brass perpetual calendar.

Copyright, Credit, and Contact

Follow Us

Our blog Dobson's Improbable History features short articles on events and people associated with each day, and updates several times each week. Get the latest on Twitter @SidewiseThinker.

Sources and Art Credits

Primary research source is Wikipedia, supplemented by other sources and personal research. All art and photographs are from Wikimedia Commons unless otherwise identified, and are either in the public domain or used under a Creative Commons license. Attribution is provided where requested by the copyright owner or when of historical significance, listed below.

- Cover photograph "Erupting, Against Dark Sky, 'Old Faithful,' Yellowstone National Park, Wyoming" by Ansel Adams comes from the National Archives and Records Administration's collection of Ansel Adams

Photographs of National Parks and Monuments, in the public domain.

- Painting of Old Faithful, Yellowstone National Park, by Albert Bierstadt, approx. 1881-1886, is in the public domain because its copyright has expired.

- The photograph of a Bulgarian martenitsa was taken by Petko Yotov, and is licensed under the Creative Commons Attribution-Share Alike 3.0 Unported license.

- The Welsh flags for St. David's Day, 2009, were photographed for the National Assembly for Wales, and are licensed under the Creative Commons Attribution 2.0 Generic license.

- The engraving "Witchcraft at Salem Village" comes from William A. Craft's *Pioneers in the Settlement of America* (1876), and is in the public domain.

- The painting *The Rape of the Sabine Women* by Peter Paul Rubens is in the public domain. The original is in the National Museum of Fine Arts, Buenos Aires, Argentina.

- The photograph of the Castle Bravo thermonuclear explosion at Bikini Atoll is in the public domain.

- The aerial photograph of Rio de Janeiro is by "Klaus with K" and is licensed under the terms of the Creative Commons Attribution-Share Alike 3.0 Unported License.

- The cover of the first issue of *Mad* Magazine is under copyright, but this low-resolution image is used under "fair use" doctrine to illustrate the importance of publisher William Gaines.

- Publicity photo of Fonzie and Ritchie from *Happy Days* is in the public domain as a publicity photograph released without copyright notice.

- The photograph of Roger Daltrey was taken by Jean-Luc Ourlin in 1976, and is licensed under the Creative Commons Attribution-Share Alike 2.0 Generic license.

- The photograph of Clinton, Rabin, and Arafat at the White House was taken by the official White House photographer and is in the public domain.

- The photograph of Chris Weber at the NBA Asia Challenge, 2010, was taken by "inboundpass" and licensed under the Creative Commons Attribution 2.0 Generic license.

- The photograph of Charlie Chaplin and Jackie Coogan in *The Kid* is in the public domain because its copyright has expired.

- The photograph of the Polaroid Land Camera is by "Morven," and licensed under the Creative Commons Attribution-Share Alike 3.0 Unported license.

- The illustration of the month of March is from the French Gothic illuminated manuscript *Les Très Riches Heures du duc de Berry* by the Limbourg Brothers, Jean Colombe, and an intermediate painter whose name is lost to history.

- The photograph of aquamarine has been released into the public domain.

- The photograph of daffodils is by Myrabella, and is licensed under the Creative Commons Attribution-Share Alike 3.0 Unported license.

- The 1917 Women's Suffrage demonstration comes from the Library of Congress, Prints and Photographs Division, LC-USZ62-31799 DLC

- The photograph of the 2012 Mardi Gras Night Parade was taken by Mills Baker, licensed under the Creative Commons Attribution 2.0 Generic License.

- The 50-year perpetual calendar photograph is in the public domain.